# Vegan Instant Pot

— — — — — ❧❧❧❧ — — — — —

## The Essential Quick and Simple Vegan Cookbook for Weight Loss and Clean Eating

**Brandon Parker**

Additionally, the information in the following pages is intended only for informational purposes and should thus be thought of as universal. As befitting its nature, it is presented without assurance regarding its prolonged validity or interim quality. Trademarks that are mentioned are done without written consent and can in no way be considered an endorsement from the trademark holder.

# Introduction

Thank you for getting a copy of "**Vegan Instant Pot: The Essential Quick and Simple Vegan Cookbook for Weight Loss and Clean Eating**."

One of the biggest advantages of using the **Instant Pot** is that meals can be cooked quickly. The process entails pouring in the ingredients, pressing a few buttons, and letting the machine do the rest. There's no need to spend long hours in the kitchen watching over the pot, or waiting for a particular dish to cook so that it can be depressurized manually.

If you've ever used a stovetop pressure cooker, you'd know exactly what happens with an unwatched pot. Let's just say, no one appreciates a lid being accidentally embedded in the ceiling.

The **Instant Pot** works particularly well with dried ingredients like: beans, grains, legumes, and/or pulses. Instead of pre-soaking these for 2 to 12 hours prior to cooking, these ingredients can be placed directly into the crockpot of the machine, along with the recommended amount of liquids. At high pressure, these could be cooked in less than 30 minutes.

This book contains basic guidelines on how to use the **Instant Pot** for everyday cooking. It contains tips on how to buy and prepare ingredients in the fastest way possible, and how to store cooked dishes for later consumption.

This book also contains the easiest, most delectable, pressure-cooked vegan-safe recipes for any meal of the day. These are healthy selections that use fresh ingredients for maximum

Introduction

flavor. There are a few lightly processed ingredients included (e.g. dried herbs, canned mushrooms, frozen fruits, etc.) that help make food preparation go faster.

Thanks again for downloading this book. I hope you enjoy it.

# Contents

# Chapter 1:

# **Instant Pot Pressure Cooker Basics**

**Instant Pot** is a multi-function, countertop 11 psi electric cooker. It can be used as a rice cooker, slow cooker, steamer, warmer, and pressure cooker. Newer models like IP-DUO and IP-SMART have: browning, pasteurization, sautéing, and yogurt making functions.

**Instant Pot** machines come in three sizes: five, six, and eight quarts. Machines with large capacities are best for making homemade steamed bread and yogurt.

These can be used for pasteurizing milk and for making cheeses. These are also suitable for making large meals for parties, or if you want to freeze large volumes of dishes (e.g. broths, soups, stews, etc.) for later consumption.

Each **Instant Pot** comes with a crockpot (stainless steel inner pot/sleeve,) a removable lid with steaming vent, steaming basket, and a removable trivet.

## Benefits of using Instant Pot

1. This is the quintessential set-it-and-walk-away all-in cooker. All you need to do is to:

   - Prepare the ingredients beforehand. Place these into the crockpot.
   - Twist and lock the lid. Seal or unseal steamer valve (depending on function.)
   - Set desired function (e.g. PRESSURE COOK, STEAM, etc.). Set the timer.
   - Walk away and return after the prescribed cooking time. (See **Note.**)
   - Release the pressure. Remove the lid.
   - Stir in remaining ingredients, if any.
   - Ladle dish into serving containers. Garnish as needed. Serve. Eat.

**Note**: **Instant Pot** has a "KEEP WARM" (warming) function, which automatically activates after the timer goes off. Unless it is specified in the recipe(s) that you need to turn off the machine *immediately after cooking,* there is no need to rush back to the cooker. You can return to the kitchen whenever you want.

2. Pressure cooking means that you can cook meals 75% to 100% faster than boiling/braising on the stovetop, and baking/roasting in a conventional oven.

   This is especially helpful for vegan meals that entail the

use of dried beans, legumes, pulses, etc. Instead of pre-soaking these ingredients for hours prior to use, you can pour these directly into the crockpot, add water, and pressure cook these for several minutes. (See **Appendix I** for recommendations.)

3. Use **Instant Pot** to make meals in advance. The machine automatically activates the KEEP WARM function after each cooking cycle. This allows you to prepare meals in the morning, so that you can come home to a warm dinner. Or, set up the **Instant Pot** before going to bed so that breakfast is cooked when you wake up.

## How to use the Instant Pot

**Instant Pot** has automatic: BEAN/CHILI, MEAT/STEW, MULTIGRAIN, PORRIDGE, POULTRY, PRESSURE, RICE, SAUTE, SLOW COOK, SOUP, STEAM, WARM, and YOGURT functions. (See **Appendix II**.)

For this book, we will concentrate on how to use the PRESSURE or pressure cooker function.

The two easiest ways to do so is to:

**Step 1**:

1. Pour all the ingredients into the crockpot.

2. Close lid. Twist it to lock. Beeping sounds will indicate if machine is sealed.

3. Seal valve (steaming vent) on top of the lid by turning the knob towards the SEALING option (the opposite of which is VENTING.) By doing so, the machine automatically assumes that you are opting for NATURAL PRESSURE RELEASE. This means that the

lid remains sealed until the pressure within the crockpot dissipates or lessens, extending the cooking time by up to 20 minutes.

4. Press the PRESSURE (pressure cooker) button.

5. Wait for 10 seconds without doing anything. The machine will automatically go to its preset option, which is at: HIGH PRESSURE at 30 minutes.

6. After the cooking cycle, and the NATURAL PRESSURE RELEASE, the machine will automatically activate the KEEP WARM function.

7. This is the only time you can safely open the lid.

## Step 2:

1. Pour all the ingredients into the crockpot.

2. Close lid. Twist it to lock. Seal valve.

3. Set machine on MANUAL mode. This still means that you are still pressure cooking, but you can change settings.

4. Choose either LOW PRESSURE or HIGH PRESSURE button. Most of the time though, dishes need to be cooked on high pressure.

5. Set the timer by pushing the plus [ + ] or minus [ - ] buttons right above the PRESSURE button, to increase or decrease cooking time, respectively.

6. Wait for 10 seconds without doing anything. The machine will then start cooking according to your "instructions."

7. If the recipe calls for turning off the machine immediately after cooking, press the KEEP WARM button twice to CANCEL after the cooking cycle. Or, you can simply unplug the machine.

8. If the recipe recommends QUICK PRESSURE RELEASE, carefully turn the knob on the lid towards VENTING. Keep your face and hands away from the steam as it comes out to prevent second-degree burns. Depending on how much moisture is inside the crockpot, venting can take between fifteen seconds to five minutes.

9. Only when the steam has subsided can you safely open the lid.

Sealing = valve is closed. Steam cannot escape, which allows pressure to build up within. NATURAL PRESSURE RELEASE means waiting for pressure to subside on its own for 15 to 20 minutes. In the meantime, the pressure cooker remains sealed.

Venting = valve is manually opened. This is called QUICK PRESSURE RELEASE. After steam is released (1 to 2 minutes,) the pressure cooker can be opened immediately.

There are some recipes that require additional steps (e.g. browning, liquid reduction, etc.), so it is best to follow the recommended procedure when cooking.

**Important: Instant Pot** should have at least one cup of liquid during cooking to prevent contents from sticking to the bottom of the crockpot.

If recipes for pressure cooking require large volumes of liquid, pour in just enough to fill 2/3 of the crockpot. This is to ensure that there is space for pressure and steam to build up within.

For other cooking functions, never fill the pot over the MAX line indicator to avoid spillage.

If you made a mistake with the settings, or you simply want to add a few more ingredients to the crockpot, double press the KEEP WARM button to CANCEL. Opt for a QUICK PRESSURE RELEASE and wait for the steam to subside, if any. Reset the machine as needed.

For other functions and more details: check product manual.

# Chapter 2.

# Breakfast

## 01 Apple-Cinnamon Quinoa

Prep Time: 10 minutes; Cook Time: 11 minute

Recommended Serving Size: 1 cup: Serves 4

Ingredients:

- 2 cups water
- 1 cup brown or red quinoa, rinsed well, drained
- ½ cup peeled, diced apple
- ¼ cup brown sugar, add more if desired
- ¼ tsp. cinnamon powder
- ½ cup rice or soy milk, add more if desired

## Chapter 2: Breakfast

Garnishes

- ½ cup peeled apple, sliced into ½-inch thick half-moons, sprinkled with...
- ¼ tsp. freshly squeezed lemon juice

Directions:

1. To make garnishes, place half-moon apples in bowl. Sprinkle with lemon juice to prevent browning. Set aside. Drain before using.

2. Except for garnishes and milk, stir in remaining ingredients into crockpot.

3. Close lid, lock, and seal valve.

4. **Press: MANUAL** on the machine, and then **HIGH**. Set the timer at **1 minute.**

5. When timer beeps, opt for NATURAL PRESSURE RELEASE, approximately 10 minutes. Turn off machine. Remove lid.

6. Stir in milk. Taste. Adjust seasoning if needed.

7. Spoon equal portions of cooked quinoa into bowls. Garnish with a few slices of half-moon apples. Cool slightly before serving.

8. To store leftovers, place quinoa (sans garnishes) in a microwave oven-safe container. Store in the fridge for up to three days. This can be consumed cold.

   Or, if desired, reheat quinoa in the microwave oven at highest heat setting for 10 to 15 seconds. Stir in more milk. Add fresh garnishes.

**Note**: the best apple cultivars to use in this recipe are: cameo, empire, Fuji, gala, golden delicious, Granny Smith, honey crisp, Jonagold, McIntosh, and sweet tango.

## 02 Chickpeas on Yogurt

Prep Time: 5 minutes; Cook Time: 5 minutes

Recommended Serving Size: ½ cup of cooked chickpeas; Serves 4 to 6

Ingredients:

- 1 Tbsp. coconut oil
- 1 Tbsp. minced garlic
- ½ cup minced shallot
- 1 can 15 oz. chickpeas, rinsed, drained well
- 1 cup **Mushroom and Vegetable Broth, Unsalted**
- ¼ tsp. coconut butter
- ¼ cup freshly toasted pine nuts
- 2 Tbsp. freshly squeezed lemon juice
- 2 Tbsp. minced fresh cilantro
- 1 Tbsp. raw sugar or agave sugar

Spice Mix

- ½ tsp. Spanish paprika
- ¼ tsp. chili powder
- ¼ tsp. cumin powder
- ¼ tsp. kosher salt
- ⅛ tsp. turmeric powder

- 1/16 tsp. black pepper
- 1/16 tsp. cayenne pepper powder
- 1/16 tsp. cinnamon powder

Flavor base

- ½ cup of coconut, rice, or soy yogurt per person, chilled well prior to use

Directions:

1. Press: SAUTÉ, and HIGH.

2. Pour oil into crockpot. Wait until oil has warmed through. Sauté onion until limp.

3. Stir in chickpeas and spice mix until well blended.

4. Except for cilantro, lemon juice, and pine nuts, stir in remaining ingredients.

5. Close lid, lock, and seal valve.

6. Press: MANUAL, HIGH, and 5 minutes.

7. When timer beeps, slide valve open for QUICK PRESSURE RELEASE. Turn off machine. Remove lid.

8. Stir in lemon juice and pine nuts. Taste. Adjust seasoning only if needed. Cool slightly before proceeding.

9. Pour chilled yogurt into cups.

10. Spoon over ½ cup of cooked chickpeas on top.

11. Garnish with small amount of cilantro just before serving.

12. To store leftovers, place cooked chickpeas (sans yogurt) in a microwave oven-safe container. Store in the fridge for up to three days. Reheat chickpeas in the microwave oven on highest heat setting for 20 seconds.

13. Alternately, ladle chickpeas over a bed of freshly cooked rice, or on a freshly toasted vegan-safe bread. Serve immediately.

**Note**: if you prefer cooking your own chickpeas, pre-cook one cup an hour before. See for instructions.

# 03 Cold Tomato Soup with Cashew Cheese

Prep Time: 10 minutes; Cook Time: 5 minutes

Recommended Serving Size: 1 cup: Serves 4

Ingredients:

- 1 can 24 oz. tomato juice
- 1 can 15 oz. whole corn kernels, rinsed, drained
- 1 Tbsp. tomato puree
- 1 cup **Mushroom and Vegetable Broth, Unsalted**
- ½ cup cubed red bell pepper
- ½ cup cubed zucchini
- ¼ cup diced green onions
- ¼ tsp. kosher salt, add more later if desired
- 1/16 tsp. black pepper

Garnishes

- ½ cup Homemade Cashew Cheese at room temperature
- ½ cup loosely packed fresh alfalfa sprouts, rinsed, spun-dried

Directions:

1. Except for garnishes, pour ingredients into crockpot.

2. Close lid, lock, and seal valve.

3. **Press: MANUAL, HIGH, and 5 minutes**.

4. When timer beeps, slide valve open for QUICK PRESSURE RELEASE. Remove lid. Stir in cashew cheese. Taste. Adjust seasoning if needed.

5. Ladle soup into bowls. Garnish with alfalfa sprouts just before serving.

6. Alternately, let soup come to room temperature. Ladle into a non-reactive container and chill for at least 6 hours prior to use. Serve cold without alfalfa. This dish should be consumed immediately.

# 04 Corn and Quinoa

Prep Time: 10 minutes; Cook Time: 11 minute

Recommended Serving Size: 1 cup: Serves 4

Ingredients:

- 2 Tbsp. olive oil
- 1½ cups **Mushroom and Vegetable Broth, Unsalted**
- 1 cup quinoa, picked over, but do not rinse
- 1 cup water
- ¼ cup minced chives
- 1 can 15 oz. whole corn kernels, rinsed, drained
- 1/16 tsp. kosher salt
- 1/16 tsp. white pepper, optional

# Chapter 2: Breakfast

Directions:

1. Press: SAUTÉ, and HIGH.

2. Pour oil into crockpot. Wait until oil has warmed through. Stir-fry quinoa until this releases a nutty aroma.

3. Except for chives, stir in remaining ingredients into the crockpot.

4. Close lid, lock, and seal valve.

5. Press: MANUAL, HIGH, and 1 minute.

6. When timer beeps, opt for NATURAL PRESSURE RELEASE, approximately 10 minutes. Remove lid.

7. Taste. Adjust seasoning only if needed.

8. Ladle equal portions into plates. Garnish with chives. Serve immediately.

9. Store leftovers (sans chives) in the fridge. This will keep for two days at the most. Reheat in the microwave oven on highest heat setting for 10 seconds.

# 05 Crunchy Chocolate Steel-Cut Oatmeal

Prep Time: 5 minutes; Cook Time: 23 minutes

Recommended Serving Size: ¾ cup: Serves 4

Additional equipment: pastry brush

Ingredients:

- 1½ Tbsp. coconut butter or coconut oil
- 4 cups water
- 1 cup steel-cut oats (don't use instant or quick-cooking oats)
- 2 Tbsp. brown sugar, add more if desired
- 1 Tbsp. pure cocoa powder

Garnishes

- 1 cup almond milk, add more if desired
- ½ cup store-bought, unbleached almond slivers, freshly toasted on a dry pan
- ½ cup vegan-safe chocolate buttons or chips

Directions:

1.  Using a pastry brush, lightly grease insides of crockpot.

2.  Except for garnishes, pour in ingredients.

3.  Close lid, lock, and seal valve.

4.  **Press: MANUAL, HIGH, and 13 minutes**.

5.  When timer beeps, opt for NATURAL PRESSURE RELEASE, approximately 10 minutes. Turn off machine. Remove lid.

6.  Stir in milk. Taste. Adjust seasoning if needed.

7.  Ladle oatmeal into bowls. Garnish with almond slivers and chocolate buttons. Cool slightly before serving.

8.  Store leftovers (sans garnishes) in the fridge for up to two days. Serve cold or reheat in the microwave oven on highest heat setting for 15 seconds. Stir in more milk if oatmeal becomes clumpy. Add fresh garnishes, if desired.

**Note**: substitute any vegan-safe milk or any nuts of choice. Omit nuts if desired. Substitute dried fruits like banana chips, raisins, or prunes.

# 06 Fresh Berries on Quinoa

Prep Time: 10 minutes; Cook Time: 11 minute

Recommended Serving Size: ¾ cup with berries: Serves 4

Ingredients:

- 2 cups water
- 1 cup quinoa, rinsed well, drained
- ⅛ cup white sugar, add more if desired
- 1/16 tsp. cinnamon powder
- 1/16 tsp. nutmeg powder

Garnishes:

- 1 cup hulled fresh strawberries, roughly chopped, divided
- ½ cup fresh blueberries, divided
- ½ cup rice or soy milk
- 1 drop vanilla extract

Directions:

1. Except for toppings, pour remaining ingredients into crockpot.

2. Close lid, lock, and seal valve.

3. **Press: MANUAL, HIGH, and 1 minute**.

4. When timer beeps, opt for NATURAL PRESSURE RELEASE, approximately 10 minutes. Remove lid.

5. Stir in half of blueberries, and half of strawberries, along with milk and vanilla extract. Taste. Adjust seasoning if needed.

6. Spoon equal portions of cooked quinoa into bowls. Garnish with more blueberries and strawberries. Cool slightly before serving.

7. To store leftovers, place quinoa (sans garnishes) in a microwave oven-safe container. Store in the fridge for up to three days. This can be consumed cold. Or, if desired, reheat quinoa in the microwave oven on highest heat setting for 15 seconds. Stir in more milk. Add fresh garnishes.

**Note:** substitute any fresh or seasonal berries of choice. If using frozen berries, thaw and lightly drain these before using.

# 07 Fruity and Nutty Steel-Cut Oatmeal

Prep Time: 5 minutes; Cook Time: 23 minutes

Recommended Serving Size: ¾ cup: Serves 4

Additional equipment: pastry brush

Ingredients:

- 1½ Tbsp. coconut butter or coconut oil
- 4 cups water
- 1 cup steel-cut oats (don't use instant or quick-cooking oats)
- ¼ cup white sugar, add more later if desired

Garnishes

- 1 cup frozen blueberries, no need to thaw
- ½ cup store-bought, lightly-salted toasted walnuts, crumbled
- ½ cup walnut milk or any vegan-safe milk substitute of choice

Directions:

1. Using a pastry brush, lightly grease the insides of the crockpot.

2. Pour oats, sugar, and water into crockpot. Stir.

3. Close lid, lock, and seal valve.

4. **Press: MANUAL, HIGH, and 13 minutes**.

5. When timer beeps, opt for NATURAL PRESSURE RELEASE, approximately 10 minutes. Remove lid.

6. Stir in frozen blueberries and milk. Residual heat will partially thaw berries.

7. Taste. Adjust seasoning if needed.

8. Ladle oatmeal into bowls. Garnish with walnuts. Cool slightly before serving.

9. To store leftovers, place cooked oats (sans garnishes) in a microwave oven-safe container. Store in the fridge for up to three days. This can be consumed cold. Or, if desired, reheat in the microwave oven on highest heat setting for 15 seconds. Stir in more milk. Add fresh garnishes.

**Note**: substitute any frozen berries or nuts of choice. Omit nuts, if desired. If using dried fruits (e.g. apricots, cranberries, mangoes, prunes, raisins, etc.), add these to the crockpot with the oats prior to cooking. Add ¼ cup more water to the recipe.

# 08 Okayu (Japanese Style Porridge)

Prep Time: 20 minutes; Cook Time: 20 minutes

Recommended Serving Size: 1 cup: Serves 4

Ingredients:

- 4 cups water
- ¼ cup jasmine rice, rinsed well, drained

Garnishes

- 4 small pieces *umeboshi* or pickled plum (one piece per person)
- 1 Tbsp. toasted sesame seeds
- ¼ cup minced chives
- ¼ cup shredded *nori* or Japanese seaweed
- kosher salt, only if needed

Directions:

1. Except for garnishes, pour remaining ingredients into crockpot.

2. Close lid, lock, and seal valve.

3. **Press: MANUAL, HIGH, and 5 minutes**.

4. When timer beeps, opt for NATURAL PRESSURE RELEASE, approximately 15 minutes.

5. Ladle porridge into bowls. Add desired amount of garnishes. Season according to taste. Cool slightly before serving.

6. Store leftover porridge (sans garnishes) in the freezer for up to one week. Thaw well. Reheat in the microwave oven on highest heat setting for 30 seconds. Stir in 10 second intervals. Garnish prior to serving.

# 09 Scrambled "Eggs" on Toast

Prep Time: 25 minutes; Cook Time: 2 to 3 minutes

Recommended Serving Size: ¾ cup of seasoned tofu and 1 slice of bread; Serves 4

Additional equipment: cheesecloth, colander

Ingredients:

- 1 freshly toasted, thick-cut vegan bread per person
- 2 packs 12 oz. extra firm tofu, wrapped tightly in cheesecloth, and pressed / squeezed to remove excess moisture, set aside in a colander to drain for at least 15 minutes prior to use, remove from cheesecloth, crumbled

Seasonings

- 2 Tbsp. olive oil
- 2 Tbsp. **Homemade Cashew Cheese**, add more later if desired
- 1 Tbsp. minced garlic

- ½ cup minced onion
- ½ cup **Mushroom and Vegetable Broth, Unsalted**
- ¼ cup diced red bell pepper
- ¼ cup diced and deseeded tomatoes
- ⅛ cup minced green onions
- ¼ tsp. kosher salt
- ¼ tsp. turmeric powder
- 1/16 tsp. black pepper
- 4 small sprigs parsley, for garnish, optional

Directions:

1. Press: SAUTÉ, and HIGH.

2. Pour oil into crockpot. Wait until oil has warmed through. Sauté garlic, onion, and tomatoes until limp.

3. Except for cashew cheese, green onions, and parsley, stir in remaining ingredients.

4. Close lid, lock, and seal valve.

5. Press: MANUAL, HIGH, and 1 minute.

6. When timer beeps, slide valve open for QUICK PRESSURE RELEASE. Remove lid.

7. Stir in cashew cheese and green onions. Taste. Adjust seasoning if needed.

8. Spoon "scrambled eggs" on toasted bread. Garnish with parsley sprigs. Serve.

9. Alternately, serve with hash browns or steamed brown rice.

10. Store leftovers (sans garnishes) in the fridge for up to three days. Lightly drain before reheating in a lightly oiled non-stick pan, to maintain that "eggy" texture. Add more cheese if desired.

**Note**: leftovers can also be stir-fried in fried rice.

If you have time, or you would like to make more tofu "raw eggs," place several blocks of pressed / squeezed tofu in the freezer for 3 to 24 hours. Thaw and drain well before using. This step firms up the tofu, and makes it absorb seasonings better.

# 10 Vegan Jook (Rice Congee with "Scallops")

Prep Time: 5 minutes; Cook Time: 20 minutes

Recommended Serving Size: 1 cup: Serves 4

Ingredients:

- 2 cups Mushroom and Vegetable Broth, Unsalted
- 2 cups water
- ¼ cup jasmine rice, rinsed well, drained
- ½ pound king oyster stems, trimmed well, sliced into inch thick disks
- ⅛ tsp. kosher salt, add more if desired
- 1/16 tsp. white pepper, optional
- ¼ cup minced green onions, for garnish

Directions:

1. Except for green onions, pour ingredients into crockpot.

2. Close lid, lock, and seal valve.

3. **Press: MANUAL, HIGH, and 5 minutes**.

4. When timer beeps, opt for NATURAL PRESSURE RELEASE, approximately 15 minutes.

5. Stir. Taste. Adjust seasoning if needed.

6. Ladle congee into bowls. Garnish with small amount of green onions. Cool slightly before serving.

7. Store leftover porridge (sans garnishes) in the freezer for up to one week. Thaw well. Reheat in the microwave oven on highest heat setting for 30 seconds. Stir in 10 second intervals. Garnish prior to serving.

# Chapter 3.

# **Lunch Ideas**

## **01 Easy Quinoa Salad**

Prep Time: 10 minutes; Cook Time: 11 minute

Recommended Serving Size: 1 cup: Serves 4

Ingredients:

- 2 Tbsp. olive oil
- 1 cup **Mushroom and Vegetable Broth, Unsalted**
- 1 cup quinoa, picked over, but do not rinse
- 1 cup water
- 1 small piece lime, sliced into wedges
- ¼ pound arugula, rinsed, drained, roughly torn
- ⅛ pound cherry tomatoes, sliced into wedges, lightly drained
- 1/16 tsp. balsamic vinegar
- 1/16 tsp. red pepper flakes
- Kosher salt, only if needed

Directions:

1. Press: SAUTÉ, and HIGH.

2. Pour oil into crockpot. Wait until oil has warmed through. Stir-fry quinoa until this releases a nutty aroma.

3. Stir in broth and water into crockpot.

4. Close lid, lock, and seal valve.

5. Press: MANUAL, HIGH, and 1 minute.

6. When timer beeps, opt for NATURAL PRESSURE RELEASE, approximately 10 minutes. Turn off machine. Remove lid. Cool slightly before proceeding.

7. Stir in balsamic vinegar, cherry tomatoes, and red pepper flakes.

8. Taste. Add salt only if needed.

9. Arrange desired amount of arugula on plates.

10. Spoon equal portions of quinoa salad on top.

11. Serve with lime wedges. Squeeze lime juice over salad just before eating.

**Note**: this dish is versatile. Add any ingredient you wish, such as: lightly toasted nuts or seeds, fresh mango slivers, or steamed asparagus. This should be consumed immediately.

Any dark, flavorful, vinegar can be used in lieu of the balsamic vinegar. Try black currant, date, malt, or persimmon vinegar.

Add fresh chilies, if desired.

# 02 Chickpea and Fennel Couscous

Prep Time: 10 minutes; Cook Time: 5 minutes

Recommended Serving Size: 1 cup: Serves 6

Ingredients:

- 1 Tbsp. olive oil
- ½ small fennel, bulb thinly sliced, reserve tops for garnish
- 1 can 15 oz. chickpeas, rinsed, drained
- ½ cup pitted black Kalamata olives in brine, drained well
- 2 cups couscous pearls (not instant)
- 1 cup **Mushroom and Vegetable Broth, Unsalted**
- 1 cup water
- ¼ cup freshly squeezed lemon juice
- Salt, only if needed

Directions:

1. Press: SAUTÉ, and HIGH.

2. Pour oil into crockpot. Wait until oil has warmed through. Sauté fennel bulb until seared brown.

3. Except for fennel fronds and lemon juice, stir in remaining ingredients into the crockpot.

4. Close lid, lock, and seal valve.

5. Press: MANUAL, HIGH, and 5 minutes.

6. When timer beeps, slide valve open for QUICK PRESSURE RELEASE. Turn off machine.

7. Using a fork, stir in lemon juice. Taste. Add salt only if needed.

8. Ladle equal portions on plates. Garnish with dill fronds. Serve. This dish should be consumed immediately.

## 03 Green Pea Soup

Prep Time: 20 minutes; Cook Time: 10 minutes

Recommended Serving Size: 1 cup: Serves 4

Additional Equipment: immersion blender

Ingredients:

- 1½ Tbsp. olive oil
- ½ cup julienned shallots
- 1½ pounds frozen baby peas (no need to thaw)
- 2 cups **Mushroom and Vegetable Broth, Unsalted**
- 2 cups water
- ½ cup **Homemade Cashew Cheese**, reserve half for garnish
- ¼ tsp. kosher salt, add more later if desired
- 1/16 tsp. white pepper
- 3 large fresh mint, thinly sliced, for garnish

Directions:

1. Press: SAUTÉ, and HIGH.

2. Pour oil into crockpot. Wait until oil has warmed through. Sauté onion until limp.

3. Except for cashew cheese and mint, stir in remaining ingredients into crockpot.

4. Close lid, lock, and seal valve.

5. Press: MANUAL, HIGH, and 5 minutes.

6. When timer beeps, slide valve open for QUICK PRESSURE RELEASE. Remove lid.

7. Stir in half of cashew cheese. Taste. Adjust seasoning only if needed. Cool slightly before proceeding.

8. Puree soup using an immersion blender until smooth.

9. Ladle soup into bowls. Garnish with small amount of cashew cheese and mint leaves before serving.

10. Store leftovers (sans garnishes) in the freezer for up to one week. Reheat in the microwave oven on highest heat setting for 30 seconds, stirring in 10 second intervals.

# 04 Quick and Easy Coconut and Squash Soup

Prep Time: 20 minutes; Cook Time: 10 minutes

Recommended Serving Size: 1 cup: Serves 4

Additional Equipment: immersion blender

Ingredients:

- 1½ to 2 pounds butternut squash, peeled, deseeded, cubed
- 2 cups **Mushroom and Vegetable Broth, Unsalted**
- 1 15 oz. can of thick coconut cream, divided
- 1 piece bird's eye chili, deseeded, minced, optional
- 1 tsp. onion powder
- ⅛ tsp. cayenne pepper powder, optional
- ½ tsp. garlic powder
- ¼ tsp. kosher salt, add more later only if needed
- ⅛ tsp. white pepper
- Water
- ¼ cup fresh chives, minced, for garnish

Directions:

1. Except for chives, coconut cream, and water, pour ingredients into crockpot.

2. Half-fill with water.

3. Close lid, lock, and seal valve.

4. **Press: MANUAL, HIGH, and 20 minutes**.

5. When timer beeps, slide valve open for QUICK PRESSURE RELEASE. Remove lid.

6. Pour in ¾ of coconut cream. Using an immersion blender, process soup until smooth. Taste. Adjust seasoning only if needed.

7. Ladle equal portions of soup into bowls. Add dollops (approximately 1 tsp.) of leftover coconut cream. Garnish with fresh chives. Cool slightly before serving.

8. Store leftovers in the freezer (sans garnishes) for three days or (sans coconut cream and garnishes) for up to one week. Reheat in the microwave oven on highest heat setting for 30 seconds, stirring in 10 second intervals.

# 05 Ratatouille in 6 Minutes

Prep Time: 20 minutes; Cook Time: 6 minutes

Recommended Serving Size: 1 cup: Serves 4

Ingredients:

- ¾ cup of cooked wild rice per person, keep warm
- 2 Tbsp. olive oil, divided
- 1 Tbsp. minced garlic
- 1 cup diced yellow onion
- 1 cup **Mushroom and Vegetable Broth, Unsalted**
- 1 cup diced eggplant
- 1 cup diced summer squash
- ½ cup diced red bell pepper
- ½ cup diced zucchini
- 1 8 oz. can chickpeas, rinsed, drained well
- 3 Tbsp. tomato sauce
- 1 Tbsp. tomato paste
- ¼ Tbsp. brown sugar
- ¼ tsp. kosher salt, add more only if needed

- ¼ cup fresh basil leaves, rinsed, squeezed dry, roughly chopped
- 4 small thyme sprigs, for garnish

Directions:

1. Press: SAUTÉ, and HIGH.

2. Pour oil into crockpot. Wait until oil has warmed through. Sauté garlic and onion until limp and aromatic.

3. Except for basil, rice, and thyme, stir in remaining ingredients into the crockpot.

4. Close lid, lock, and seal valve.

5. Press: MANUAL, HIGH, and 5 minutes.

6. When timer beeps, slide valve open for QUICK PRESSURE RELEASE. Turn off machine. Remove lid.

7. Stir in basil leaves. Taste. Adjust seasoning only if needed.

8. Place equal portions of ratatouille and cooked rice on plates. Garnish with thyme. Serve immediately.

**Note**: this recipe works better if vegetables are sliced almost uniformly in size. If desired, substitute canned button mushrooms (pieces and stems,) cannellini beans, green peas, or whole corn kernels for the chickpeas. Or, simply do without.

This dish should be consumed immediately.

# 06 Spicy Pepper Soup

Prep Time: 30 minutes; Cook Time: 6 minutes

Recommended Serving Size: 1 cup: Serves 6

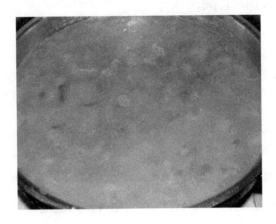

Ingredients:

- One thick slice of any crusty, vegan-safe bread per person
- 2 Tbsp. olive oil
- 2 Tbsp. minced garlic
- 1 cup chopped white onion
- 2 cups **Mushroom and Vegetable Broth, Unsalted**
- 1 cup diced red bell pepper, deseeded
- 1 cup diced acorn squash, peeled and deseeded
- 1 cup diced yellow squash, peeled and deseeded
- 1 cup diced zucchini, unpeeled
- 1 cup water
- ½ cup diced Anaheim or Poblano chilies, deseeded
- 1 large piece diced fresh jalapeno pepper, deseeded
- 1 can 15 oz. whole corn kernels, rinsed, drained
- 1 can 15 oz. pinto beans, rinsed, drained
- ½ tsp. cayenne powder

- ½ tsp. sweet paprika powder
- ½ tsp. coriander powder
- ¼ tsp. brown sugar, optional
- ¼ tsp. kosher salt, add more later if desired
- ⅛ tsp. black pepper

Directions:

1. Press: SAUTÉ, and HIGH.

2. Pour oil into crockpot. Wait until oil has warmed through. Sauté garlic and onion until limp and transparent.

3. Except for bread, pour in remaining ingredients.

4. Press: MANUAL, HIGH, and 5 minutes.

5. When timer beeps, slide valve open for QUICK PRESSURE RELEASE. Turn off machine. Remove lid.

6. Taste. Adjust seasoning only if needed.

7. Ladle soup into bowls. Serve with crusty bread on the side.

8. Store leftovers (sans bread) in the freezer for up to one week. Reheat in the microwave oven on highest heat setting for 30 seconds, stirring in 10 second intervals.

# 07 Summer Soup with Almonds

Prep Time: 20 minutes; Cook Time: 5 minutes

Recommended Serving Size: 1½ cups: Serves 10

Ingredients:

- One thick slice of any crusty, vegan-safe bread per person
- 2 cups **Mushroom and Vegetable Broth, Unsalted**
- 1 cup cauliflower florets, sliced into bite-sized pieces
- 1 cup spinach leaves, rinsed, spun-dried, roughly torn
- 1 cup almond milk, optional
- ½ cup carrot, sliced into ½-inch thick half-moons
- ½ cup diced potato
- ½ cup frozen peas
- ½ cup almond slivers, freshly toasted on a dry pan
- ¼ cup roughly chopped fresh parsley, for garnish
- ½ tsp. kosher salt, add more later if desired
- ⅛ tsp. white pepper
- ⅛ tsp. Spanish paprika powder
- 1/16 tsp. oregano powder

- 1/16 tsp. rosemary powder
- Water

Directions:

1. Except for almond slivers, bread, basil, milk, parsley, and water, pour remaining ingredients into crockpot.

2. Pour water until crockpot is 2/3 full. Stir.

3. Close lid, lock, and seal valve.

4. **Press: MANUAL, HIGH, and 5 minutes**.

5. When timer beeps, slide valve open for QUICK PRESSURE RELEASE. Turn off machine. Remove lid.

6. Stir in almond milk and basil. Taste. Adjust seasoning only if needed.

7. Ladle soup into bowls. Garnish with almond slivers and parsley. Serve with a slice of crusty bread on the side.

8. Store leftovers (sans bread and garnishes) in the freezer for up to five days. Reheat in the microwave oven on highest heat setting for 30 seconds, stirring in 10 second intervals. Add fresh garnish just prior to serving.

# 08 Three Mushroom Soup

Prep Time: 20 minutes; Cook Time: 7 to 10 minutes

Recommended Serving Size: 1½ cups: Serves 6 to 10

Ingredients:

- One thick slice of any crusty, vegan-safe bread per person
- 3 Tbsp. olive oil, divided
- ½ cup julienned white onion
- 2 cups **Mushroom and Vegetable Broth, Unsalted**
- 1 cup butternut squash, peeled, halved/quartered lengthwise, wavy cut into ½-inch thick half-moons
- 1 cup carrots, peeled, halved lengthwise, wavy cut into ½-inch thick half-moons
- ½ cup packed baby spinach leaves, rinsed, spun-dried, roughly torn
- ¼ cup packed dried wood ear fungus, soaked in warm water for 30 minutes, rinsed, drained well, torn to bite-sized pieces

- ¼ pound fresh oyster mushroom, cleaned well using paper towels, roots trimmed, halved or quartered to bite-sized pieces
- ¼ pound white *enoki* mushrooms, roots trimmed, individual stems separated
- ¼ tsp. kosher salt, add more later if desired
- 1/16 tsp. white pepper, optional
- 2 sprigs fresh parsley, roughly chopped, for garnish, optional
- Water

Directions:

1. Press: SAUTÉ, and HIGH.

2. Pour 1 Tbsp. of oil into crockpot. Wait until oil has warmed through. Sauté onion until limp and transparent.

3. Except for bread, pour in remaining oil into crockpot, along with *enoki* and oyster mushrooms. Stir-fry until everything is lightly seared, and most of the moisture from mushrooms have evaporated. This would take approximately 2 to 5 minutes.

4. Except for basil, parsley, and water, stir in remaining ingredients.

5. Pour water until crockpot is 2/3 full. Stir.

6. Close lid, lock, and seal valve.

7. Press: MANUAL, HIGH and 5 minutes.

8. When timer beeps, slide valve open for QUICK PRESSURE RELEASE. Turn off machine. Remove lid.

9. Stir in basil. Taste. Adjust seasoning only if needed.

10. Ladle soup into bowls. Garnish with parsley. Serve with a slice of crusty bread on the side.

11. Store leftovers (sans bread and garnishes) in the freezer for up to one week. Reheat in the microwave oven on highest heat setting for 30 seconds, stirring in 10 second intervals.

## 09 Too Easy Split Pea Soup

Prep Time: 10 minutes; Cook Time: 16 to 17 minutes

Recommended Serving Size: 1 cup: Serves 4

Ingredients:

- ¼ cup vegan-safe croutons or cubed and toasted bread per person
- 1 Tbsp. olive oil
- 1 pound dried yellow split peas, picked over
- ½ cup minced white onion
- 1 cup diced carrots
- ¼ cup diced celery stalks
- 2 pieces medium fresh bay leaves
- ½ tsp. kosher salt
- ⅛ tsp. white pepper
- 4 cups water
- 2 cups **Mushroom and Vegetable Broth, Unsalted**

Directions:

1.  Press: SAUTÉ, and HIGH.

2.  Pour oil into crockpot. Wait until oil has warmed through. Sauté onion until limp.

3.  Except for croutons, stir in remaining ingredients.

4.  Close lid, lock, and seal valve.

5.  Press: MANUAL, HIGH, and 15 minutes.

6.  When timer beeps, slide valve open for QUICK PRESSURE RELEASE. Turn off machine. Remove lid.

7.  Stir. Taste. Adjust seasoning only if needed.

8.  Ladle equal portions of soup into cups. Garnish with desired amount of croutons, if using. Cool slightly before serving.

9.  Store leftovers (sans croutons) in the fridge for up to two days. Reheat in the microwave oven on highest heat setting for 30 seconds, stirring in 10 second intervals.

# 10 Vegetable Curry with Mushrooms

Prep Time: 30 minutes; Cook Time: 11 minutes

Recommended Serving Size: ¾ cup curry with ½ cup of rice; Serves 4 to 6

Ingredients:

- ½ cup cooked brown rice per person
- 2 Tbsp. minced garlic
- 1 Tbsp. coconut oil
- 1 Tbsp. grated ginger, drained
- 1 Tbsp. tomato paste
- 2 cups **Mushroom and Vegetable Broth, Unsalted**
- 1 cup minced onion
- 1 cup cubed potato
- 1 cup cubed squash
- 1 cup water
- ½ cup cubed carrot
- ½ cup red bell pepper
- ½ cup cubed sweet potato
- 1 piece banana chili, halved, deseeded
- 1 piece bird's eye chili, halved, deseeded,

- 2 cans 15 oz. thick coconut cream, divided
- 1 can 8 oz. straw mushrooms, halved lengthwise, rinsed, drained well
- 1 can 8 oz. whole button mushrooms, rinsed, drained, quartered
- 2 Tbsp. fresh alfalfa sprouts, for garnish

Spice Mix

- 1 Tbsp. brown sugar
- 1 Tbsp. curry powder
- ½ Tbsp. *garam masala*
- ½ tsp. Spanish paprika
- ¼ tsp. cinnamon powder
- ¼ tsp. cumin powder
- ¼ tsp. kosher salt
- ¼ tsp. red pepper flakes
- ⅛ tsp. black pepper
- ⅛ tsp. coriander powder
- ⅛ tsp. turmeric powder

Directions:

1. Combine spice mix in a bowl. Set aside.
2. **Press: SAUTÉ, and HIGH.**
3. Pour oil into crockpot. Wait until oil has warmed through. Sauté garlic, ginger and onion until limp and aromatic.
4. Stir in spice mix until well blended.
5. Except for alfalfa sprouts, cooked rice, and one can of coconut cream, stir in remaining ingredients.
6. Close lid, lock, and seal valve.

7. **Press: MANUAL, HIGH, and 10 minutes**.

8. When timer beeps, slide valve open for QUICK PRESSURE RELEASE. Turn off machine. Remove lid.

9. Stir in last can of coconut cream. Taste. Adjust seasoning only if needed.

10. Ladle equal portions of curry into a bowl. Garnish with small amount of alfalfa sprouts. Serve with cooked brown rice on the side.

11. Store leftovers (sans garnish and rice) in the freezer for up two days at the most. Reheat in the microwave oven on highest heat setting for 20 seconds. Serve with freshly cooked rice on the side.

# Chapter 4:

# Dinner / Main Course

## 01 Almonds in Sautéed Squash

Prep Time: 20 minutes; Cook Time: 10 minutes

Recommended Serving Size: 1 cup: Serves 4

Ingredients:

- 1 Tbsp. olive oil
- 1 cup **Mushroom and Vegetable Broth, Unsalted**
- ½ cup almond slivers, freshly toasted on a dry pan, for garnish
- ¼ cup minced white onion
- ⅛ cup minced chives, for garnish
- 1 pound cubed butternut squash
- 1 pound French beans, ends and strings removed, sliced into 2-inch long slivers
- ¼ tsp. kosher salt
- 1/16 tsp. white pepper

Directions:

1. Press: SAUTÉ, and HIGH.

2. Pour oil into crockpot. Wait until oil has warmed through. Sauté onion until limp.

3. Except for almonds, chives, and French beans, stir in ingredients into crockpot.

4. Close lid, lock, and seal valve.

5. Press: MANUAL, HIGH, and 10 minutes.

6. When timer beeps, slide valve open for QUICK PRESSURE RELEASE. Remove lid.

7. Stir in French beans. Secure lid for 2 minutes to warm French beans through.

8. Taste. Adjust seasoning if needed.

9. Ladle equal portions of vegetables into plates. Garnish with almond slivers and chives. This dish should be consumed immediately.

## 02 Black Bean and Rice Casserole

Prep Time: 20 minutes; Cook Time: 36 minutes

Recommended Serving Size: 1 cup: Serves 6

Ingredients:

- ¼ cup olive oil
- 1 cup minced shallot
- 1 Tbsp. minced garlic
- ½ Tbsp. oregano powder
- 1 pound dried black beans, picked over (no need to soak)
- 1 large piece minced fresh jalapeño pepper, deseeded
- 1 tsp. kosher salt, add more later if desired

Garnishes

- 4 cups cooked brown rice, forked through to loosen grains, approximately one cup per person
- ½ cup loosely packed, roughly chopped cilantro
- ½ cup freshly juiced lime

Directions:

1.  Press: SAUTÉ, and HIGH.

2.  Pour oil into crockpot. Wait until oil has warmed through. Sauté garlic and shallot until limp and transparent.

3.  Except for garnishes, stir in remaining ingredients into crockpot.

4.  Close lid, lock, and seal valve.

5.  Press: MANUAL, HIGH, and 25 minutes.

6.  When timer beeps, opt for NATURAL PRESSURE RELEASE, approximately 10 minutes. Turn off machine. Remove lid.

7.  Using a fork, stir in rice and lime juice. Taste. Adjust seasonings, if needed.

8.  Ladle equal portions on plates. Garnish with cilantro. Serve.

9.  Store leftovers (sans garnishes) in the fridge for two days at the most. Reheat in the microwave oven on highest heat setting for 10 seconds.

# 03 Braised Brussel Sprouts with Toasted Peanuts

Prep Time: 20 minutes; Cook Time: 4 minutes

Recommended Serving Size: 1 cup: Serves 4

Ingredients:

- ¾ cup of cooked white rice per person
- 1½ pounds Brussels sprouts, bottoms trimmed, halve larger pieces
- ½ Tbsp. palm sugar
- ½ Tbsp. peanut oil
- ⅛ cup water
- ¼ tsp. fresh lemon zest
- ⅛ tsp. black pepper, add more if desired
- ⅛ tsp. kosher salt, only if needed
- 3 Tbsp. freshly squeezed lemon juice
- ¼ cup roasted, lightly salted (low-sodium) peanuts, store-bought

Directions:

1. Except for lemon juice, peanuts, rice, and salt, pour ingredients into crockpot.

2. Close lid, lock, and seal valve.

3. **Press: MANUAL, HIGH, and 4 minutes**.

4. When timer beeps, slide valve open for QUICK PRESSURE RELEASE. Turn off machine. Remove lid.

5. Pour in lemon juice. Stir in salted peanuts. Taste. Add salt only if needed.

6. Ladle equal portions of braised vegetables into plates with steamed rice on the side. Serve immediately. This dish should be consumed immediately.

## 04 Braised Green and Red Cabbage in Sweet and Spicy Sauce

Prep Time: 20 minutes; Cook Time: 11 to 13 minutes

Recommended Serving Size: 1½ cups loosely packed: Serves 4

Ingredients:

- ¾ cup of cooked white rice per person
- 2 Tbsp. coconut oil, add more only if needed
- 2 pounds green cabbage, sliced into 8 wedges, slice off thicker parts of the core but do not completely remove
- 1½ pounds red cabbage, sliced into 8 wedges, slice off thicker parts of the core but do not completely remove
- 1 cup water
- 1 cup diced potatoes
- ½ cup grated carrots
- ¼ cup **Mushroom and Vegetable Broth, Unsalted**
- ¼ cup coconut vinegar
- 1 tsp. brown sugar
- ½ tsp. cayenne powder

- ½ tsp. red pepper flakes
- ½ tsp. kosher salt
- ⅛ tsp. roasted sesame oil
- ¼ cup loosely packed fresh parsley tops, roughly torn

Cornstarch slurry

- 2 tsp. cornstarch dissolved in...
- 2 Tbsp. water

Directions:

1. Press: SAUTÉ, and HIGH.

2. Pour 1 Tbsp. of oil into crockpot. Wait until oil has warmed through.

3. Frying in batches, brown cabbage wedges on cut sides. Temporarily transfer partially cooked cabbages to a plate. Repeat step for all cabbage wedges. Pour in more oil when crockpot becomes too dry.

4. Except for cornstarch slurry, parsley, rice, sesame oil, and salt, place remaining ingredients (including cabbages) into the crockpot.

5. Close lid, lock, and seal valve.

6. Press: MANUAL, HIGH, and 5 minutes.

7. When timer beeps, slide valve open for QUICK PRESSURE RELEASE. Remove lid.

8. Arrange vegetables on a serving platter. Leave most of the cooking liquid in the crockpot.

9. To make gravy, press: SAUTÉ, and HIGH.

10. Stir in cornstarch slurry. Cook until gravy thickens. Turn off machine.

11. Stir in salt and sesame oil. Taste. Adjust seasoning if needed.

12. Place equal amounts of cooked vegetables and cooked rice on plates.

13. Ladle gravy on top of veggies. Garnish with fresh parsley. This dish should be consumed immediately.

## 05 Creamy Mushroom and Potato Risotto with Fresh Arugula

Prep Time: 30 minutes; Cook Time: 18 to 19 minutes

Recommended Serving Size: 1 cup rice: Serves 4

Ingredients:

- 1 Tbsp. olive oil
- 1 large piece onion, peeled, minced
- ½ pound fresh button/Portabella mushrooms, roots trimmed, caps thinly sliced
- 1½ cups Arborio rice, rinsed, drained well
- 1 medium piece waxy potato, diced
- 1 Tbsp. tomato paste
- ¼ cup white wine
- 2 cups **Mushroom and Vegetable Broth, Unsalted**
- 2 cups water
- 1/16 tsp. kosher salt
- ¼ tsp. dried thyme
- ½ cup **Homemade Cashew Cheese**, add more if desired
- ¼ pound fresh arugula/rocket leaves, rinsed, drained, torn to bite-sized pieces

Directions:

1. Press: SAUTÉ, and HIGH.

2. Pour oil into crockpot. Wait until oil has warmed through. Sauté onion until limp.

3. Stir-fry mushrooms until seared brown.

4. Stir in rice.

5. Except for arugula and cashew cheese, pour in remaining ingredients.

6. Close lid, lock, and seal valve.

7. Press: MANUAL, HIGH, and 5 minutes.

8. When timer beeps, opt for NATURAL PRESSURE RELEASE, approximately 15 minutes. Turn off machine. Remove lid.

9. Remove crockpot from machine to prevent rice from overcooking.

10. Stir in cashew cheese. Taste. Adjust seasoning if needed.

11. Ladle equal portions of risotto into serving plates. Top off with equal portions of fresh arugula leaves. Cool slightly before serving.

12. Store leftovers (sans garnishes) in the freezer for two days at the most. Reheat in the microwave oven on highest heat setting for 30 seconds, stirring in 10 second intervals. Add fresh garnishes, if desired.

# 06 Green Mung Bean Stew with Squash

Prep Time: 30 minutes; Cook Time: 18 to 20 minutes

Recommended Serving Size: ½ cup of stew with ¾ cup of rice: Serves 4

Ingredients:

- ¾ cup of cooked brown or wild rice per person
- 2 Tbsp. coconut oil
- 1 Tbsp. grated garlic
- ½ cup minced shallot
- ½ cup minced red tomatoes
- 1½ cups *mung* beans, picked over, rinsed, drained
- 2 cups water
- 2 cups **Mushroom and Vegetable Broth, Unsalted**
- 2 cups cubed butternut squash
- ½ cup bitter melon, halved, deseeded, scrape off white inner lining, sliced diagonally into ¼-inch thick slivers, optional
- ¼ tsp. kosher salt
- ⅛ tsp. black pepper
- ¼ cup fresh *moringa* or chili leaves, rinsed, drained, optional

Directions:

1. Press: SAUTÉ, and HIGH.

2. Pour oil into crockpot. Wait until oil has warmed through. Sauté garlic and onion until limp and aromatic.

3. Stir in tomatoes. Cook until tomatoes are soft and wilted. This would take between 3 to 5 minutes.

4. Except for *moringa* leaves and rice, pour in remaining ingredients into crockpot.

5. Close lid, lock, and seal valve.

6. Press: MANUAL, HIGH, and 15 minutes.

7. When timer beeps, slide valve open for QUICK PRESSURE RELEASE. Turn off machine. Remove lid.

8. Stir in *moringa* leaves. Residual heat will cook these through.

9. Taste. Adjust seasoning if needed.

10. Place cooked rice into deep bowls. Make a well in the center.

11. Pour stew into well. Cool slightly before serving.

12. Store leftovers (sans garnishes and rice) in the fridge for up to one week. Reheat in the microwave oven on highest heat setting for 30 seconds, stirring in 10 second intervals. Serve with freshly cooked rice.

## 07 Quinoa Tabbouleh

Prep Time: 20 minutes; Cook Time: 17 to 20 minutes

Recommended Serving Size: 1 cup: Serves 4

Ingredients:

- 2 Tbsp. olive oil
- 1 Tbsp. minced garlic
- 1 small piece, eggplant, halved lengthwise, sliced into ¼-inch thick half-moons
- 1 cup **Mushroom and Vegetable Broth, Unsalted**
- 1 cup quinoa, picked over, but do not rinse
- 1 cup water
- ¼ cup red bell pepper, sliced into ¼-inch thick slivers
- 1/16 tsp. white pepper, optional

Garnishes

- 6 to 8 small pieces parsley tops, for garnish
- 2 Tbsp. minced fresh mint
- 1 cup cherry or plum tomatoes, quartered, deseeded

- ⅛ cup freshly squeezed lemon juice
- 1 medium piece shallot, julienned
- 1/16 tsp. kosher salt, add more later only if needed

Directions:

1. Combine shallot and salt in a small bowl. Mash well so that shallot releases a lot of moisture. Set aside for 5 minutes. Rinse. Drain well.

2. **Press: SAUTÉ, and HIGH.**

3. Pour oil into crockpot. Wait until oil has warmed through. Stir-fry quinoa until this releases a nutty aroma.

4. Stir in garlic, eggplant and red bell pepper. Cook until vegetables are wilted.

5. Except for garnishes, stir in remaining ingredients into the crockpot.

6. Close lid, lock, and seal valve.

7. **Press: MANUAL, HIGH, and 5 minutes.**

8. When timer beeps, opt for NATURAL PRESSURE RELEASE, approximately 10 minutes. Turn off machine. Remove lid.

9. Except for parsley tops, stir in remaining ingredients, including shallots.

10. Taste. Add more salt only if needed.

11. Place equal portions into plates. Garnish with parsley tops. This dish should be consumed immediately.

# 08 Sautéed Mushroom Congee

Prep Time: 20 minutes; Cook Time: 21 minutes

Recommended Serving Size: 1 cup: Serves 4

Ingredients:

- 2 cups Mushroom and Vegetable Broth, Unsalted
- 2 cups water
- 1 cup fresh button or oyster mushroom caps, cleaned well using paper towels, diced
- ¼ cup jasmine rice, rinsed well, drained
- ½ cup diced onion
- ¼ cup diced carrots
- ¼ cup minced green onions
- 1½ Tbsp. coconut oil
- 2 Tbsp. minced garlic
- 1 Tbsp. minced ginger
- ⅛ tsp. kosher salt, add more if desired
- 1/16 tsp. white pepper, optional
- 4 small pieces curly parsley tops, for garnish

Directions:

1. Press: SAUTÉ, and HIGH.

2. Pour oil into crockpot. Wait until oil has warmed through. Sauté garlic, ginger, and onion until limp and aromatic.

3. Stir-fry mushrooms until lightly seared.

4. Except for green onions and parsley, stir in remaining ingredients into crockpot.

5. Close lid, lock, and seal valve.

6. Press: MANUAL, HIGH, and 5 minutes.

7. When timer beeps, opt for NATURAL PRESSURE RELEASE, approximately 15 minutes.

8. Stir in green onions. Taste. Adjust seasoning if needed.

9. Ladle congee into bowls. Garnish with parsley. Cool slightly before serving.

10. Store leftovers (sans garnishes) in the freezer for up to one week. Reheat in the microwave oven on highest heat setting for 30 seconds, stirring in 10 second intervals.

## 09 Spicy Red Lentils Stew

Prep Time: 7 minutes; Cook Time: 26 to 31 minutes

Recommended Serving Size: ¾ cup: Serves 4

Ingredients:

- 2 Tbsp. coconut oil
- ½ cup minced shallot
- 1½ cup red or brown lentils, picked over
- 6 cups of water
- 4 cups packed fresh kale leaves, ribs removed, torn to bite-sized pieces, rinsed, squeezed dry
- 2 cups **Mushroom and Vegetable Broth, Unsalted**
- ¼ cup diced carrots, optional
- ⅛ cup diced red bell pepper, optional
- 1 tsp. kosher salt, add more later if needed
- ⅛ tsp black pepper, add more later if desired
- 4 Tbsp. freshly squeezed lemon juice

Spice Mix

- 2 tsp. coriander powder
- 1 tsp. garlic powder
- ½ tsp. cinnamon powder

- ½ tsp. turmeric powder
- ¼ tsp. cardamom powder
- ¼ tsp. cayenne powder
- ¼ tsp. clove powder
- ¼ tsp. nutmeg powder
- ¼ tsp. red chili flakes

Directions:

1. Press: SAUTÉ, and HIGH.

2. Pour oil into crockpot. Wait until oil has warmed through. Sauté shallot until limp and aromatic.

3. Stir in the spice mix and lentils until well blended.

4. Pour in water and broth.

5. Except for kale leaves, and lemon juice and stir in remaining ingredients into crockpot.

6. Close lid, lock, and seal valve.

7. Press: MANUAL, HIGH and 10 minutes.

8. When timer beeps, opt for NATURAL PRESSURE RELEASE, approximately 15 to 20 minutes.

9. Stir in kale leaves and lemon juice. Taste. Adjust seasoning if needed.

10. Ladle stew into bowls. Cool slightly before serving.

11. Store leftovers in the freezer for two days at the most. Reheat in the microwave oven on highest heat setting for 30 seconds, stirring in 10 second intervals.

## 10 Tomato-Broccoli Couscous Casserole

Prep Time: 20 minutes; Cook Time: 5 minutes

Recommended Serving Size: 1 cup: Serves 6

Ingredients:

- 3 Tbsp. olive oil
- 1 Tbsp. minced garlic
- ½ cup minced shallots
- 2 cups couscous pearls (not instant)
- 1 cup **Mushroom and Vegetable Broth, Unsalted**
- 1 cup water
- ¼ cup freshly squeezed lemon juice
- ¼ cup fresh mint, roughly chopped
- 1 pound fresh and firm tomatoes, cubed

Spice mix

- ½ tsp. sweet paprika powder
- ¼ tsp. kosher salt
- ⅛ tsp. red chili flakes
- ⅛ tsp. white pepper

- 1/16 tsp. cardamom powder
- 1/16 tsp. cinnamon powder
- 1/16 tsp. coriander powder
- 1/16 tsp cumin powder
- 1/16 tsp. ginger powder
- 1/16 tsp. turmeric powder

Directions:

1. Press: SAUTÉ, and HIGH.

2. Pour oil into crockpot. Wait until oil has warmed through. Sauté garlic and onion until limp and transparent.

3. Except for lemon juice, mint leaves, and fresh tomatoes, stir in remaining ingredients (including spice mix) into crockpot.

4. Close lid, lock, and seal valve.

5. Press: MANUAL, HIGH, and 5 minutes.

6. When timer beeps, slide valve open for QUICK PRESSURE RELEASE. Turn off machine. Remove lid.

7. Stir in lemon juice. Taste. Adjust seasoning if needed.

8. Ladle equal portions on plates. Garnish with fresh mint and tomatoes. This dish should be consumed immediately.

# Chapter 5:.

# **Desserts**

## 01 Berry Sauce in a Flash

Prep Time: 5 minutes; Cook Time: 10 minutes

Recommended Serving Size: ¼ cup; Multiple servings

Additional equipment: immersion blender

Ingredients:

- ½ cup rice ice cream per person
- 2 cups frozen hulled strawberries, thawed, do not drain
- 2 cups frozen blackberries or blueberries, thawed, do not drain
- 2 cups frozen cranberries or raspberries, thawed, do not drain
- 1 cup water
- ½ cup brown sugar, add more if desired
- 1 piece vanilla bean, halved lengthwise
- 1 tsp. freshly squeezed lemon juice
- ½ cup dried coconut shavings, for garnish, optional

- ½ cup freshly toasted walnuts, crumbled, for garnish, optional

Directions:

1. Except for coconut, ice cream, lemon juice, and walnuts, place ingredients into crockpot.

2. Close lid, lock, and seal valve.

3. **Press: MANUAL, HIGH, and 10 minutes**.

4. When timer beeps, slide valve open for QUICK PRESSURE RELEASE. Remove lid. Cool slightly before proceeding.

5. Stir in lemon juice. Discard spent vanilla bean. Taste. Adjust seasoning only if needed.

6. Puree fruit sauce using an immersion blender. Chill well before serving.

7. Pour chilled fruit sauce on top of rice ice cream. Garnish with small amount of coconut shavings and crumbled walnuts, if using. Serve immediately.

8. Store leftovers (sans garnishes) in the fridge for up to one week. Serve as needed.

# 02 Brown Rice Pudding

Prep Time: 20 minutes; Cook Time: 23 to 25 minutes

Recommended Serving Size: 1 cup: Serves 4

Ingredients:

- 3 cups water
- 1 cup almond milk
- 1 cup jasmine rice, rinsed well, drained
- ¼ cup brown sugar

Garnishes

- ¼ cup raisins
- Cinnamon powder

Directions:

1. Except for almond milk and garnishes, pour ingredients into crockpot. Stir.

2. Close lid, lock, and seal valve.

3. **Press: MANUAL, HIGH, and 5 minutes**.

4. When timer beeps, opt for NATURAL PRESSURE RELEASE, approximately 15 minutes. Remove lid. Stir in almond milk.

5. **Press: SAUTÉ and HIGH**.

6. Cook pudding until most of the liquid has evaporated. Turn off machine.

7. Ladle pudding into bowls. Garnish with small amount of raisins and dash of cinnamon powder. Cool slightly before serving.

8. Store leftovers (sans garnishes) in the fridge for two days at the most. Reheat in the microwave oven on highest heat setting for 20 seconds, stirring in 10 second intervals. Pour in more warmed almond milk if pudding gets too clumpy or thick. Add fresh garnishes, if desired.

# 03 Crockpot Carrot "Cake"

Prep Time: 15 minutes; Cook Time: 20 minutes

Recommended Serving Size: ¾ cup: Serves 6

Additional Equipment: pastry brush

Ingredients:

- 1 Tbsp. coconut butter or coconut oil
- 4 cups water
- 1 cup packed grated carrots
- 1 cup steel cut oats
- ½ cup raisins
- ¼ cup chia seeds
- 3 Tbsp. maple syrup, add more if desired
- ½ tsp. cinnamon powder
- ¼ tsp. all spice powder
- ¼ tsp. ginger powder
- ¼ tsp. nutmeg powder
- ⅛ tsp. clove powder
- 1/16 tsp. kosher salt

Garnishes

- 1 cup walnut milk
- ½ cup shelled, toasted walnuts, lightly-salted, crumbled

Directions:

1. Using a pastry brush, lightly grease insides of crockpot with coconut butter.

2. Except for chia seeds and garnishes, pour ingredients into crockpot. Stir.

3. Close lid, lock, and seal valve.

4. **Press: MANUAL, HIGH and 10 minutes**.

5. When timer beeps, slide valve open for QUICK PRESSURE RELEASE. Turn off machine. Remove lid.

6. Stir in chia seeds. Secure lid. Set aside for another 10 minutes. Porridge should be thick. Taste. Adjust seasoning if needed.

7. Ladle porridge into bowls. Garnish with small amount of walnuts.

8. Drizzle walnut milk just before eating. Serve while warm.

9. Store leftovers (sans walnut milk) in the fridge for three days at the most. Serve chilled. Add more walnut milk, if desired.

**Note**: Other substitutes for walnuts and walnut milk are: almond slivers, and almond milk, cashew nuts and cashew milk, and chopped hazelnuts and hazelnut milk.

# 04 Mangoes and Cashew Cream

Prep Time: 1 hour and 15 minutes; Cook Time: 1 minute

Recommended Serving Size: ½ cup; Serves 8

Additional equipment: non-reactive lidded container

Ingredients:

- 12 to 15 large pieces ripe or slightly overripe mangoes, peeled, roughly chopped
- 1 small piece vanilla pod, halved lengthwise
- ½ cup water
- ¼ cup white sugar

Cashew cream

- ¼ cup Homemade Cashew Cheese
- ¼ cup store-bought cashew milk

Directions:

1. Whisk cashew cheese and cashew milk in a small bowl until frothy. Chill in the fridge until needed.

2. Place remaining ingredients into crockpot.

3. Close lid, lock, and seal valve.

4. **Press: MANUAL, HIGH, and 1 minute**.

5. When timer beeps, slide valve open for QUICK PRESSURE RELEASE. Turn off machine. Cool mangoes to room temperature before transferring to a non-reactive lidded container.

6. Chill mangoes in the fridge for an hour before serving.

7. Spoon mangoes into cups. Top off with small amount of cashew cream.

8. Store leftover mangoes in the freezer for up to one week, and cashew cream in the fridge for up to three days. Thaw mango pudding lightly before serving again. Serve with cashew cream.

**Note**: substitute the same amount of peaches for the mangoes, if desired. Kiwi fruits and strawberries work with this recipe too. Add ½ cup of sugar to lessen the tartness. Use other nut-based milk substitutes for the milk and cheese, like: almonds, hazelnuts, macadamia nut, and walnuts.

# 05 Pineapple and Plantain Pudding

Prep Time: 20 minutes; Cook Time: 20 minutes

Recommended Serving Size: 1 cup: Serves 4

Ingredients:

- 2 medium almost ripe plantains, preferably *Cardaba* or *Saba* cultivars, peeled, halved diagonally
- 2 cups ripe pineapple wedges
- 2 cups water
- 1 cup brown sugar

Directions:

1. Pour ingredients into crockpot.
2. Close lid, lock, and seal valve.
3. **Press: MANUAL, HIGH, and 10 minutes**.
4. When timer beeps, opt for NATURAL PRESSURE RELEASE, approximately 10 minutes. Remove lid.
5. Ladle pudding into bowls. Cool slightly before serving.

6. Store leftovers in the fridge for up to one week. Reheat in the microwave oven on highest heat setting for 20 seconds, stirring in 10 second intervals. Or, serve cold right out of the fridge.

**Note**: when using larger banana cultivars, approximate one piece per person.

# 06 Purple Pudding

Prep Time: 30 minutes; Cook Time: 15 minutes

Recommended Serving Size: 1 cup: Serves 8

Ingredients:

- 4 cups water
- 2 cans 15 oz. each thick coconut cream, divided
- 2 cups ripe plantains, sliced into 2-inch thick disks
- 1½ cups cubed purple yam
- 1 cup cubed ripe jackfruit
- 1 cup cubed sweet potato
- 1 cup cubed taro root
- 1 cup glutinous rice, shaped into bite-sized balls
- ½ cup brown sugar, add more if needed
- ½ cup seed tapioca pearls, rinsed, drained well (no need to soak)

Directions:

1. Except for one can of coconut cream, pour ingredients into crockpot. Stir.

2. Close lid, lock, and seal valve.

3. **Press: MANUAL, HIGH, and 5 minutes**.

4. When timer beeps, opt for NATURAL PRESSURE RELEASE, approximately 10 minutes. Remove lid.

5. Stir in remaining can of coconut cream. Taste. Adjust seasoning if needed.

6. Ladle pudding into cups. Cool slightly before serving.

7. Store leftovers in the fridge for up to one week. This dish actually tastes better chilled or cold.

# 07 Stone Fruit Sauce in a Flash

Prep Time: 1 hour and 15 minutes; Cook Time: 10 minutes

Recommended Serving Size: ¼ cup; Multiple servings

Ingredients:

- ½ cup of rice ice cream per person
- 2 cups fresh apricots, peeled, pitted, thinly sliced
- 2 cups fresh nectarines, peeled, pitted, thinly sliced
- 2 cups fresh peaches, peeled, pitted, thinly sliced
- 1 cup water
- ½ cup white sugar, add more if desired
- 1 piece vanilla bean, halved lengthwise
- ¼ tsp. cinnamon powder
- 1 tsp. freshly squeezed lemon juice

Directions:

1. Except for ice cream and lemon juice, place ingredients into crockpot.
2. Close lid, lock, and seal valve.
3. **Press: MANUAL, HIGH, and 10 minutes**.

4. When timer beeps, slide valve open for QUICK PRESSURE RELEASE. Turn off machine. Remove lid.

5. Stir in lemon juice. Discard spent vanilla bean. Taste. Adjust seasoning only if needed. Chill well (at least for an hour) before serving.

6. Pour chilled fruit sauce on top of rice ice cream. Serve immediately.

7. Store leftovers in the fridge for up to one week. Serve as needed.

# 08 Sweet Cassava Pudding

Prep Time: 5 minutes; Cook Time: 20 minutes

Recommended Serving Size: ¾ cup: Serves 6

Additional equipment: colander

Ingredients:

- 2 pounds frozen, peeled cassava or yucca, no need to thaw
- 6 cups water, divided
- 1 cup brown sugar

Directions:

1. Pour cassava and 4 cups of water into crockpot.
2. Close lid, lock, and seal valve.
3. **Press: MANUAL, HIGH, and 10 minutes**.
4. When timer beeps, slide valve open for QUICK PRESSURE RELEASE. Cool slightly before proceeding.

5. Pour contents of crockpot into colander to drain. This helps lessen or remove bitterness in cassava.

6. Return cassava to crockpot along with remaining ingredients.

7. **Press: MANUAL, HIGH, and 10 minutes**.

8. When timer beeps, slide valve open for QUICK PRESSURE RELEASE. Remove lid.

9. **Press SAUTÉ and HIGH**. Cook until most of the water has evaporated. Turn off machine.

10. Ladle cassava into bowls. Cool slightly before serving.

11. Store leftovers in the fridge for up to one week. Reheat in the microwave oven on highest heat setting for 10 to 20 seconds.

# 09 Sweet Potato Pudding

Prep Time: 10 minutes; Cook Time: 20 minutes

Recommended Serving Size: ¾ cup: Serves 6

Ingredients:

- 2 pounds sweet potatoes, peeled, cubed
- 2 cups water
- 1 cup brown sugar

Directions:

1. Pour ingredients into crockpot.

2. Close lid, lock, and seal valve.

3. **Press: MANUAL, HIGH, and 10 minutes**.

4. When timer beeps, opt for NATURAL PRESSURE RELEASE, approximately 10 minutes. Turn off machine. Remove lid. Cool slightly before proceeding.

5.  Ladle cooked sweet potatoes into bowls.

6.  Store leftovers in the fridge for up to one week. Reheat in the microwave oven on highest heat setting for 10 to 20 seconds.

# 10 Tropical Flavored Tapioca Pudding

Prep Time: 30 minutes; Cook Time: 20 minutes

Recommended Serving Size: ¾ cup: Serves 10

Ingredients:

- 4 cups water
- 1½ cups cubed ripe plantains
- 1 cup sweet potato, cubed
- 1 cup purple yam, cubed
- ½ cup cubed ripe jackfruit
- 2 cans 15 oz. each thick coconut cream, divided
- ½ cup medium or large tapioca pearls, rinsed, drained well (no need to soak)
- ¼ cup white sugar, add more if desired
- 1/16 tsp. kosher salt

Directions:

1. Except for one can of coconut cream, pour ingredients into crockpot. Stir.

2. Close lid, lock, and seal valve.

3. **Press: MANUAL, HIGH, and 10 minutes**.

4. When timer beeps, opt for NATURAL PRESSURE RELEASE, approximately 10 minutes. Remove lid.

5. Stir in remaining can of coconut cream. Adjust seasoning if needed.

6. Ladle pudding into cups. Cool slightly before serving.

7. Store leftovers in the fridge for up to one week. This dish actually tastes better chilled or cold.

# Chapter 6:

# **Snacks**

## **01 Applesauce**

Prep Time: 25 minutes; Cook Time: 15 minutes

Recommended Serving Size: ½ cup; Serves 8

Additional Equipment: masher

Ingredients:

- 10 large pieces soft-fleshed apples, peeled, cored, quartered
- 1 tsp. cinnamon powder
- ¼ tsp. nutmeg powder, optional
- ¼ cup water
- ¼ cup white sugar, add more if desired

Directions:

1. Place ingredients into the crockpot.

2. Close lid, lock, and seal valve.

3. **Press: MANUAL, HIGH, and 15 minutes**.

4. When timer beeps, slide valve open for QUICK PRESSURE RELEASE. Turn off machine. Cool slightly before proceeding.

5. Mash apples until relatively smooth (or chunky, depending on personal preference.) Taste. Adjust seasoning if needed.

6. Spoon applesauce into bowls. Serve.

7. Store leftovers in the fridge for up three days at the most. This dish actually tastes better chilled or cold.

**Note**: the best apple cultivars to use in this recipe are: Fuji, Golden Delicious, Gravenstein, Ida Red, Liberty, McIntosh, Mutsu, and Rome.

# 02 Bananas in Coconut Pudding, Thai Style

Prep Time: 10 minutes; Cook Time: 21 minutes

Recommended Serving Size: ¾ cup: Serves 4

Ingredients:

- 8 small almost ripe bananas, preferably *Namwa, Niño, or Senyorita* cultivars, peeled, quartered into 2-inch long slivers
- 1 cup water
- ¼ cup white sugar, add more later if desired
- 1 can 15 oz. thick coconut cream
- 1 Tbsp. freshly toasted sesame seeds for garnish
- 1/16 tsp. cinnamon powder

Directions:

1. Except for coconut cream and sesame seeds, pour ingredients into crockpot. Stir.
2. Close lid, lock, and seal valve.
3. **Press: MANUAL, HIGH, and 1 minute.**
4. When timer beeps, opt for NATURAL PRESSURE RELEASE, approximately 10 minutes. Remove lid.

5. Stir in remaining can of coconut cream.

6. **Press: SAUTÉ, and HIGH**.

7. Cook until sauce thickens, about 10 minutes. Turn off machine. Taste. Adjust seasoning if needed.

8. Ladle pudding into bowls. Garnish with small amount of toasted sesame seeds. Cool slightly before serving.

9. Store leftovers (sans garnishes) in the fridge for up to one week. This dish actually tastes better chilled or cold.

**Note**: when using larger banana cultivars, approximate one piece per person.

# 03 Boiled Corn on the Cob

Prep Time: 5 minutes; Cook Time: 20 minutes

Recommended Serving Size: 1 corn/person: Serves 4

Additional equipment: colander

Ingredients:

- 4 medium fresh corn on the cob, hulled, silks removed, halved to fit inside crockpot
- 4 cups water
- ¼ cup kosher salt
- ¼ cup brown sugar, optional

Directions:

1. Pour ingredients into crockpot.

2. Close lid, lock, and seal valve.

3. **Press: MANUAL, HIGH and 10 minutes**.

4. When timer beeps, opt for NATURAL PRESSURE RELEASE, approximately 10 minutes. Remove lid. Cool slightly before proceeding.

5. Pour corn into colander. Rinse with cool running water.

6. Cool slightly before serving. If desired, serve with vegan butter. This dish should be consumed immediately.

## 04 Boiled Peanuts

Prep Time: 5 minutes; Cook Time: 30 minutes

Recommended Serving Size: 1 cup: Serves 4 to 6

Additional equipment: colander

Ingredients:

- 2½ lbs. raw, unshelled peanuts, picked over, rinsed well
- 4 cups water
- 1 cup kosher salt

Directions:

1. Pour ingredients into crockpot. Close lid, lock, and seal valve.

2. **Press: MANUAL, HIGH, and 20 minutes**.

3. When timer beeps, opt for NATURAL PRESSURE RELEASE, approximately 10 minutes. Remove lid. Cool slightly before proceeding.

4. Pour peanuts into colander. Rinse with cool running water to remove most of the salt. Drain well.

5. Scoop small amount of peanuts into bowls. Shell peanuts as you eat. This dish should be consumed immediately.

# 05 Boiled Plantains

Prep Time: 2 minutes; Cook Time: 30 minutes

Recommended Serving Size: 1 piece: Serves: 6

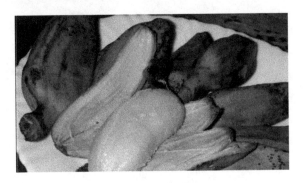

Ingredients:

- 4 cups water
- 6 fat pieces overripe and/or mushy plantains with skin on, preferably *cardaba* or *saba* cultivars as these easily fit into crockpot; if using other cultivars, halve or quarter these to fit into the pot, do not peel

Directions:

1. Pour ingredients into crockpot.
2. Close lid, lock, and seal valve.
3. **Press: MANUAL, HIGH, and 10 minutes**.
4. When timer beeps, slide valve open for QUICK PRESSURE RELEASE. Turn off machine. Remove lid.
5. Remove plantains from cooking water. Cool slightly before serving plantains in their skins. Peel just before eating. This dish should be consumed immediately.

**Note**: when boiled, some plantain cultivars will turn the cooking liquid pink, red, or purple, which will stain or darken the color of plantain flesh. This is normal. Cooked overripe plantains are naturally sweet.

# 06 Corn and Rice Pudding, Thai Style

Prep Time: 5 minutes; Cook Time: 11 minute

Recommended Serving Size: ¾ cup: Serves 6

Ingredients:

- 3 cups water
- ¾ cup Jasmine rice, rinsed, drained
- ¼ cup white sugar, add more later if desired
- 2 cans 15 oz. thick coconut cream, divided
- 1 can 15 oz. cream of corn
- 1/16 kosher salt
- ¼ cup freshly toasted coconut flakes, for garnish, optional

Directions:

1. Except for one can of coconut cream, pour ingredients into crockpot. Stir.

2. Close lid, lock, and seal valve.

3. **Press: MANUAL, HIGH, and 1 minute**.

4. When timer beeps, opt for NATURAL PRESSURE RELEASE, approximately 10 minutes. Remove lid.

5. Stir in remaining can of coconut cream. Taste. Adjust seasoning if needed.

6. Ladle pudding into bowls. Garnish with coconut flakes, if using. Cool slightly before serving. This dish should be consumed immediately.

# 07 Homemade Beet Hummus

Prep Time: 15 minutes; Cook Time: 11 minute

Recommended Serving Size: 2 Tbsp.; Multiple servings

Additional equipment: blender, rubber spatula, food-grade gloves (use these when handling beets, as its bright crimson juice stains skin)

Ingredients:

- 3 to 5 pieces vegan-safe crackers or thickly sliced cucumbers per person as base
- 6 cups water
- 2 pounds red beets, peeled
- 1 large piece peeled garlic clove

Seasonings

- 3 Tbsp. cumin powder
- 3 Tbsp. tahini
- 3 Tbsp. freshly squeezed lemon juice
- 2 Tbsp. Spanish paprika
- ¼ tsp. kosher salt, add more later if desired

Chapter 6:. Snacks

Garnishes

- 1 Tbsp. extra virgin olive oil
- 1 tsp. toasted white sesame seeds
- ¼ cup roughly chopped fresh cilantro

Directions:

1. Except for base, seasonings and garnishes, pour ingredients into crockpot.

2. Close lid, lock, and seal valve.

3. **Press: MANUAL, HIGH, and 1 minute.**

4. When timer beeps, opt for NATURAL PRESSURE RELEASE, approximately 10 minutes. Turn off heat. Remove lid. Cool slightly before proceeding.

5. Reserve 1 cup of beets' cooking liquid. Discard the rest.

6. Ladle beets into the blender, along with ½ cup of the cooking liquid, and all the seasonings. Process until smooth, scraping down the sides of the blender often. Pour one tablespoon of cooking liquid at a time to create a smooth paste. (You don't need to use all the cooking liquid.)

7. Taste. Adjust seasoning if needed.

8. Pour beet hummus into a bowl. Garnish with cilantro, olive oil, and sesame seeds. Serve with vegan-safe crackers, or sliced cucumbers.

9. Store leftovers in the fridge for up to one week. Reheat in the microwave oven on highest heat setting for 10 seconds.

10. Garnish as desired.

# 08 Homemade Hummus

Prep Time: 15 minutes; Cook Time: 30 minutes

Recommended Serving Size: 2 Tbsp.; Multiple servings

Additional equipment: blender, rubber spatula

Ingredients:

- 3 to 5 pieces vegan-safe crackers or thickly sliced cucumbers per person as base
- 6 cups water
- 1 cup dry chickpeas, picked over (no need to soak)
- 4 pieces peeled garlic cloves
- 2 pieces fresh bay leaves

Seasonings

- 3 Tbsp. tahini
- ½ cup freshly squeezed lemon juice
- ¼ tsp. cumin powder
- ¼ tsp. kosher salt, add more later if desired

Garnishes

- 2 Tbsp. extra virgin olive oil
- 1/16 tsp. toasted black sesame seeds
- 1/16 tsp. toasted white sesame seeds
- 1/16 tsp. red pepper flakes
- 1 sprig of basil

Directions:

1. Except for base, garnishes and seasonings, pour ingredients into crockpot.

2. Close lid, lock, and seal valve.

3. **Press: MANUAL, HIGH, and 20 minutes**.

4. When timer beeps, opt for NATURAL PRESSURE RELEASE, approximately 10 minutes. Remove lid. Cool slightly before proceeding.

5. Reserve 1 cup of chickpeas' cooking liquid. Discard the rest.

6. Ladle chickpeas into the blender, along with ½ cup of the cooking liquid, and all the seasonings. Process until smooth, scraping down the sides of the blender often. Pour one tablespoon of cooking liquid at a time to create a smooth paste. (You don't need to use all the cooking liquid.)

7. Taste. Adjust seasoning if needed.

8. Pour hummus into a bowl. Garnish with basil sprig, olive oil, red pepper flakes, and sesame seeds. Serve with vegan-safe crackers, or sliced cucumbers.

9. Store leftovers in the fridge for up to one week. Reheat in the microwave oven on highest heat setting for 10 seconds.

10. Garnish as desired.

# 09 Tapioca Pudding with Fresh Mangoes

Prep Time: 20 minutes; Cook Time: 15 minutes

Recommended Serving Size: ¾ cup: Serves 4

Ingredients:

- 2 cups water
- ½ cup seed tapioca pearls, rinsed, drained well (no need to soak)
- ¼ cup white sugar, add more if desired
- 2 cans 15 oz. thick coconut cream each, divided
- 1 cup diced ripe mangoes, reserve half for garnish

Directions:

1. Except for one can of coconut cream and mangoes, pour ingredients into crockpot. Stir.

2. Close lid, lock, and seal valve.

3. **Press: MANUAL, HIGH, and 5 minutes**.

4. When timer beeps, opt for NATURAL PRESSURE RELEASE, approximately 10 minutes. Remove lid.

5. Stir in remaining can of coconut cream and half of mangoes. Taste. Adjust seasoning if needed. Cool slightly before proceeding.

6. Ladle pudding into cups. Garnish with remaining mangoes.

7. Store leftovers (sans mango garnish) in the freezer for up four days at the most. This dish actually tastes better chilled or cold. Garnish with fresh mangoes before serving.

# 10 Tofu with Salted Caramel Tapioca Pearls

Prep Time: 2 minutes; Cook Time: 15 to 20 minutes

Recommended Serving Size: ¾ cup of tofu with ¼ cup caramel tapioca pearls: Serves 4

Additional equipment: colander

Ingredients:

- 2 packs 12 oz. silken or soft silken tofu, chilled well, drain just prior to serving
- 5 cups water, divided
- 1 cup seed tapioca pearls, rinsed, drained well (no need to soak)
- 1 cup brown sugar, add more if desired
- 1/16 tsp. kosher salt

Directions:

1. Pour tapioca pearls and 4 cups of water into crockpot.

2. Close lid, lock, and seal valve.

3. **Press: MANUAL, HIGH, and 5 minutes**.

4. When timer beeps, opt for NATURAL PRESSURE RELEASE, approximately 10 minutes. Turn off machine. Remove lid. Cool slightly before proceeding.

5. Pour out contents of crockpot into colander to drain.

6. **Press: SAUTÉ, and HIGH.**

7. Return tapioca pearls to crockpot. Stir in remaining ingredients.

8. Cook for 10 minutes, or until caramel thickens and tapioca pearls turn brown. Turn off machine. Cool slightly before proceeding.

9. Meanwhile, scoop drained silken tofu into heat-resistant glass or cups.

10. Pour caramel and tapioca pearls on top. Serve immediately.

11. Store caramelized tapioca pearls and tofu separately in the fridge for three days at the most. Serve cold, or briefly reheat in the microwave oven on highest heat setting for 5 to 7 seconds.

# Bonus Recipe 1:
# Homemade Cashew Cheese

Prep Time: 30 to 60 minutes; Cook Time: 15 minutes

Recommended Serving Size: ¼ cup: Multiple servings

Additional equipment: blender, cheesecloth, colander, rubber spatula, saran wrap, small spring form pan, or any suitable sized container to hold the cheese

Ingredients:

- 4 cups water
- 2 cups raw cashew nuts, picked over, no need to soak
- 1 tsp. olive oil
- 4 Tbsp. freshly squeezed lemon juice
- 4 Tbsp. nutritional yeast
- 1 tsp. kosher salt
- ½ tsp. black pepper
- ½ tsp. garlic powder

## Bonus Recipe 1: Homemade Cashew Cheese

**Note**: add any additional seasoning of choice (e.g. cayenne powder, fresh minced chives, red pepper flakes, onion powder, etc.). To prevent over salting or over seasoning the cheese, add only a quarter teaspoon at a time. Mix well after each addition.

If adding liquids (e.g. apple cider vinegar, extra virgin olive oil, honey, etc.), drizzle these on the cheese prior to serving / eating.

Directions:

1. Pour cashew nuts, oil, and water into crockpot.

2. Close lid, lock, and seal valve.

3. **Press: MANUAL, HIGH, and 5 minutes**.

4. When timer beeps, opt for NATURAL PRESSURE RELEASE, approximately 10 minutes. Turn off machine. Cool slightly before proceeding.

5. Reserve 2 cups of cooking liquid.

6. Pour contents of crockpot into colander to drain, and then pour into the blender.

7. Pulse several times to break down cashew nuts. Pour in remaining ingredients and seasonings.

8. Process cashew cheese until relatively smooth. Add a tablespoon of cooking liquid at a time, if cashew cheese is still clumpy. (You don't have to use all the cooking liquid.) Scrape down sides of blender jug in two minute intervals using a rubber spatula.

9. Turn off blender. Taste. Adjust seasoning if needed. Cashew cheese can be used immediately.

10. Alternately, pour fresh cashew cheese in a colander lined with cheesecloth.

11. Tie or twist cheesecloth ends. Press down or squeeze to remove excess moisture. Drain well.

12. Line a small spring form pan with saran wrap with long overhangs on all sides. Pour in cheese. Chill in the fridge for at least 2 hours to set. Use as needed.

# Bonus Recipe 2:

# Mushroom and Vegetable Broth, Unsalted

Prep Time: 20 minutes; Cook Time: 30 minutes

Recommended Serving Size: use as needed: Multiple servings depending on use

Additional equipment: cheesecloth, colander, stock pot, freezer-safe non-reactive lidded containers for storage

Ingredients:

- 1 Tbsp. olive oil
- ½ Tbsp. minced garlic
- 1 large piece shallot, peeled, roughly chopped
- 2 large celery stems, roughly chopped
- 2 large dried bay leaves
- 1 large piece carrot, cubed
- 1 Tbsp. apple cider vinegar

## Bonus Recipe 2: Mushroom and Vegetable Broth, Unsalted

- 1 Tbsp. freshly cracked black peppercorns
- ¼ pound dried mushrooms, presoaked in water for 30 minutes (include soaking liquid later)
- ¼ pound kitchen scraps or any wilted, leftover uncooked vegetables in the fridge or pantry (e.g. leeks, potatoes, squash, yams, etc.) peeled, deseeded, roughly chopped, optional
- water

Directions:

1. Press: SAUTÉ, and HIGH.

2. Pour oil into crockpot. Wait until oil has warmed through. Sauté garlic and onion until limp and aromatic.

3. Except for water, stir-fry remaining ingredients until lightly seared.

4. Pour water until crockpot is 2/3 full.

5. Close lid, lock, and seal valve.

6. Press: MANUAL, HIGH and 15 minutes.

7. When timer beeps, opt for NATURAL PRESSURE RELEASE, approximately 15 minutes. Turn off machine. Cool broth to room temperature for an hour for easier handling. Remove lid.

8. Line a colander with a cheesecloth. Drape this over another suitable sized stock pot. Pour in broth to strain out solids. Discard.

9. Ladle broth into small, single-serve containers. Seal. Freeze until needed.

10. Warm desired amount of broth in the microwave oven or soup pot. Season lightly just before eating.

# Appendix I

One of the best advantages of using a pressure cooker is that you can cook dried beans, legumes, pulses, etc. without the need to soak these for hours beforehand. For ingredients to cook through properly, these need to be submerge _at the very least_ under two inches of water, while making sure that the crockpot is only 2/3 full.

Dried beans, legumes, and pulses usually yield foam during the cooking process. These need that extra head room space in the pressure cooker for the foam, so it doesn't spill out of the machine. Preferably, cook only 2 cups of dried ingredients at any given time. These will bloat and double in size after cooking.

It is also advisable to add a tiny amount of fat or oil to the cooking liquid. This lessens the volume of foam without affecting the cooking time. For savory dishes, add ¼ tsp. of any cooking oil of choice. For sweet dishes, add ½ tsp. of coconut butter or coconut oil.

Lastly, always opt for a NATURAL PRESSURE RELEASE. This will prevent foam and steam from spilling over. This will add another 10 minutes to the cooking cycle.

## Appendix I

| 1 Cup of Dried Beans | Yield in Cups | Approximate Cooking Time in Minutes Under High Pressure* |
|---|---|---|
| Adzuki beans | 2 | 10 to 15 |
| Anasazi | 2¼ | 16 to 20 |
| Black (Turtle) | 2 | 16 to 21 |
| Black-Eyed (Cow) Peas | 2¼ | 5 to 7 |
| Cannellini | 2 | 18 to 21 |
| Chickpeas (Garbanzos) | 2½ | 26 to 36 |
| Christmas lima beans | 1¼ | 12 to 14 |
| Cranberry beans | 2¼ | 26 to 31 |
| Fava beans (skins must be removed after cooking, add 2 Tbsp. of oil to cooking water) | 2 | 18 to 24 |
| Flageolets | 2 | 13 to 18 |

\* Not including pressure release time

| 1 Cup of Dried Beans | Yield in Cups | Approximate Cooking Time in Minutes Under High Pressure* |
|---|---|---|
| Great Northern beans | 2¼ | 21 to 26 |
| Green peas, whole | 2 | 12 to 14 |
| Green peas, split | 2 | 4 to 6 |
| Lentils | 2 | 3 to 6 |
| Lima beans, large (add 2 Tbsp. of oil to cooking water) | 2 | 8 to 12 |
| Lima beans, baby/small | 2½ | 8 to 12 |
| Pigeon peas | 3 | 16 to 21 |
| Pinto beans | 2¼ | 18 to 21 |
| Navy beans (peas) | 2 | 12 to 21 |
| Red kidney beans | 2 | 16 to 21 |
| Scarlet runner | 1¼ | 13 to 16 |
| Soybeans (black and beige) | 2½ | 26 to 36 |

\* Not including pressure release time

If in doubt, most dried ingredients benefit more from prolonged/extended cooking.

# Appendix II

Pre-set buttons of the **Instant Pot** default to:

| Function | Heat Setting | Cook Time in Minutes |
|---|---|---|
| BEAN / CHILI | HIGH PRESSURE | 30 |
| MEAT / STEW | HIGH PRESSURE | 35 |
| MULTI-GRAIN | HIGH PRESSURE | 40 |
| PORRIDGE | HIGH PRESSURE | 20 |
| POULTRY | HIGH PRESSURE | 15 |
| PRESSURE | HIGH PRESSURE | 30 |
| RICE | LOW PRESSURE | * Depends on water volume |
| SLOW COOKER | NORMAL 90°C / 194°F to 96°C / 205°F | 240 minutes or 4 hours |
| SOUP | HIGH PRESSURE | 30 |
| STEAM | HIGH PRESSURE | 10 |

# Conclusion

Thank you once more for buying and reading, *"Vegan Instant Pot: The Essential Quick and Simple Vegan Cookbook for Weight Loss and Clean Eating."*

Creating delicious and nutritious vegan meals doesn't have to be a pain. You can simply pop a few ingredients into your **Instant Pot**, press a few buttons, and leave the kitchen for much needed rest and relaxation. When you come back, a warm dish is waiting for you.

This book contains over 50 easy-to-follow vegan-safe recipes you can use for breakfast, lunch and dinner. These utilize inexpensive but healthy ingredients that you can find in most grocery stores. Best of all, these recipes are so easy, you can create full meals, desserts, and snacks in as little as one minute!

Hopefully, by trying out some of the recipes in this book, you will be encouraged to create your own, so that you can share your vegan dishes to family and friends. This might also encourage you to try making more complicated dishes like: homemade tofu, vegan bread, etc.

Finally, if you enjoyed this book, then I'd like to ask you for a favor, would you be kind enough to leave a review for this book on Amazon? It'd be greatly appreciated!

Thank you and good luck on your health journey!

CPSIA information can be obtained
at www.ICGtesting.com
Printed in the USA
FSHW02n0721110618
49276FS

9 781542 666473